/20

# BOOM! BELLOW!! BLEAT!

## Animal Poems for Two or More Voices

Georgia Heard

Illustrated by
Aaron DeWitt

WORDSONG

AN IMPRINT OF HIGHLIGHTS
*Honesdale, Pennsylvania*

To my wise editor Rebecca M. Davis,
who hears music in words and in all creatures who *Boom*, *Bellow*, and *Bleat*
—GH

For Hunter; for those who reduce, reuse, recycle; and for conservationists
—AD

Acknowledgments
Thanks to science editor Andy Boyles for fact-checking the text.
I'm also grateful to Mark Labarr of the Vermont Audubon Society
for helping identify Northeastern forest birds in "Forest Orchestra." —GH

Text copyright © 2019 by Georgia Heard
Illustrations copyright © 2019 by Aaron DeWitt

For information about permission to
reproduce selections from this book,
contact permissions@highlights.com.

WordSong
An Imprint of Highlights
815 Church Street
Honesdale, Pennsylvania 18431
wordsongpoetry.com
Printed in China

ISBN: 978-1-62091-520-2
Library of Congress Control Number: 2018942962

First edition
10 9 8 7 6 5 4 3 2 1

The text is set in Cabin.
The illustrations are digital.

**PERFORMANCE KEY:**
The poems in this book were written to be read by two or more readers. Each reader–or group of readers–can choose one color of text to read (black or red, for example), alternating with one another. Words in blue should be spoken by all readers in unison.

# Contents

Animal Songs.................................................4

We Don't Say *Ribbit*!..............................6

We Call to Each Other..............................8

Noisy Fish...................................................10

You Can't See Us, but You Can Hear Us...12

Song Thief.................................................14

Rattlesnake Warning...........................16

Cricket Arithmetic: Three Haiku........18

Flight of the Honeybees.....................20

Bigclaw Snapping Shrimp....................22

Songsters of the Sea...........................24

The Language of Elephants......................26

Forest Orchestra.................................28

Nature's Notes.........................................30

# Animal Songs

Alligators
*Hiss*
Chimpanzees
*Hoot*
Goats
*Bleat*
Ferrets
*Dook*
Hogs
*Grunt*
Kangaroos
*Chortle*
Mosquitoes
*Whine*

Rhinoceroses
*Mmwonk*

Roosters
*Cock-a-doodle-doo*

Damselfish
*Chirp*

Moose
*Bellow*

Walruses
*Groan*

Scallops
*Cough*

Peacocks
*Scream*

Dolphins
*Whistle*

Humans

Talk Talk Talk Talk Talk Talk Talk Talk Talk

Talk Talk

Talk

Talk

Talk

Talk

# We Don't Say *Ribbit*!

I am a frog.

I am a toad.
We don't say *ribbit*!
We say . . .

*quonk*

*waaa*

*jug-o-rum*

*beeeee*

*peep*.

I am a frog.

I am a toad.

**We don't say *ribbit*!**
**We say . . .**

*twaang*

*errrrgh*

*growl*

*trill*

*yeeeeeoooow.*

I am a frog.

I am a toad.

**We don't say *ribbit*!**

# We Call to Each Other

We call to each other.

We call to each other.

Daylight is fading.

Frost powders trees.

Time to fly south for winter.

Follow the flyways,

cling to the coastline.

*Honk*

*Honk*

*Honk*

*Honk*

*Honk*

*Honk*

*Honk*

*Honk*

We call to each other.

        We call to each other.

Daylight lingers.

        Balmy air breathes on buds.

      **Time to fly north for spring.**

Follow the melting snow line,

        home to our nesting spots.

*Honk*

*Honk*

*Honk*

*Honk*

*Honk*

*Honk*

*Honk*

9

# Noisy Fish

Glub

Blub

Glug

Swish

Moan

Groan

# You Can't See Us, but You Can Hear Us

Snow has melted;
ice is thawing in the wetlands.
Listen to our spring song:

Peep Peep Peep Peep Peep Peep Peep
Peep Peep Peep Peep Peep Peep Peep
Peep Peep Peep Peep Peep Peep Peep

We chant in threes;
a bass voice opens our round.
Listen to our spring song:

Peep Peep Peep Peep Peep Peep Peep
Peep Peep Peep Peep Peep Peep Peep
Peep Peep Peep Peep Peep Peep Peep

Sun is setting;
our chorus bells the night air.
Listen to our spring song:

Peep Peep Peep Peep Peep Peep Peep
Peep Peep Peep Peep Peep Peep Peep
Peep Peep Peep Peep Peep Peep Peep

# Song Thief

Mockingbird,

Mockingbird,

why is it

why is it

what I sing

what I sing

you sing too?

you sing too?

Why is it

Why is it

on moonlit nights

on moonlit nights

**you warble like me?**
**And I warble like you?**

Song thief!

          Song thief!

Why do you

          Why do you

**steal**

my song

          my song

from my heart,   from my throat,
from my throat?  from my heart?

Why do you

          Why do you

mock me,

          mock me,

**Mockingbird?**

# Rattlesnake Warning

Stay
away;
I'm
warning
you.

*chhhhh-chhhhh-chhhhh
chhhhh-chhhhh-chhhhh
chhhhhchhhhhchhhhhchhhhhchhhhh*

By day,
no surprise,
I spy you
with my eyes.

*chhhhh-chhhhh-chhhhh
chhhhh-chhhhh-chhhhh
chhhhhchhhhhchhhhhchhhhhchhhhh*

By night,
I see your heat
as I slither
near your feet.

*chhhhh-chhhhh-chhhhh
chhhhh-chhhhh-chhhhh
chhhhhchhhhhchhhhhchhhhhchhhhh*

Stay
away;
I'm
warning
you.

*chhhhh-chhhhh-chhhhh
chhhhh-chhhhh-chhhhh
chhhhhchhhhhchhhhhchhhhhchhhhh*

I'LL BITE!

# Cricket Arithmetic: Three Haiku

On a sticky night,
crickets hide among sweet grass—
the concert begins!

chirp chirp chirp chirp chirp chirp chirp chirp chirp chirp chirp chirp chirp chirp chirp chirp chirp chirp chirp chirp chirp chirp chirp chirp chirp chirp chirp chirp chirp chirp chirp chirp chirp chirp chirp chirp chirp

In a drumming rain,
crickets huddle under ferns—
a soggy chorus.

chirp chirp chirp chirp chirp chirp chirp chirp chirp chirp chirp chirp chirp chirp chirp chirp chirp chirp chirp chirp

Cold pierces evening,
crickets crouch in corn stubble—
last chant of the year.

chirp chirp chirp chirp chirp chirp chirp chirp chirp chirp

NOTE: Can you tell what the temperature is in these verses? After performing the cricket song, count the cricket chirps, and then add forty to get the temperature for each verse.

# Flight of the Honeybees

**We** *bzzzzzzzzzzzzzzzzzzzzzzzzzzzzzzzzzzzzzzzzzzzzzzzzzz*

from flower

to flower:

cerulean snapdragon,

golden sunflower,

blush rose,

marking nectar-filled blooms with our scent.

**We** *bzzzzzzzzzzzzzzzzzzzzzzzzzzzzzzzzzzzzzzzzzzzzzzzzzzzzz*

back to our hive

and do a map dance.

**We** *bzzzzzzzzzzzzzzzzzzzzzzzzzzzzzzzzzzzzzzzzzzzzzzz*

from fruit

to fruit:

pink plum blossom,

fragrant lime flower,

fiery pomegranate bloom,

legs dusted with pollen,

honey stomachs packed with nectar.

**We** *bzzzzzzzzzzzzzzzzzzzzzzzzzzzzzzzzzzzzzzzzzzzzzzzzzzzzzzzzzzz*

back to our hive

to fill our honey pots.

20

**We** *bzzzzzzzzzzzzzzzzzzzzzzzzzzzzzzzzzzzzzzzzzzzzzzzzzzzzzzzzzzzzzz*

from vegetable

to vegetable:

lacy onion orb,

pale celery parasols,

yellow-petalled broccoli.

**We** *bzzzzzzzzzzzzzzzzzzzzzzzzzzzzzzzzzzzzzzzzzzzzzzzzzzzzzzzz*

back to our hive.

We bzzzzzzzzzz.

We bzzzzzzzzzz.

We bzzzzzzzzzz.

We bzzzzzzzzzz.

with our wings,

Fanning nectar

## we concoct our golden honey!

# Bigclaw Snapping Shrimp

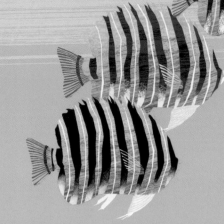

Scuttling along the sea flat floor,

        a shrimp the size of a pointer finger

burrows into a sandy hole,

        peers up at fish swimming by,

lifts its jumbo claw and . . .

snap . . .

# BANG!

Fish,fishswimawayfast,

watchoutforshrimp'sbubbleblast!

# Songsters of the Sea

I dive
down deep
in a sapphire sea.

Suspended,
I sing
an aria.

*WOOOOOOOO*

*WOOOOOOOO*

*WOOOOOOOO*

*WOOOOOOOO*

My watery hymn
serenades humpback whales
thousands of miles away.

Like an echo,
I hear a whale sing
my song back to me.

*WOOOOOOOO*

*WOOOOOOOO*

*WOOOOOOOO*

*WOOOOOOOO*

We warble.

We moan.

We trill.

We croon.

**We harmonize.**

**We are
songsters of the sea.**

24

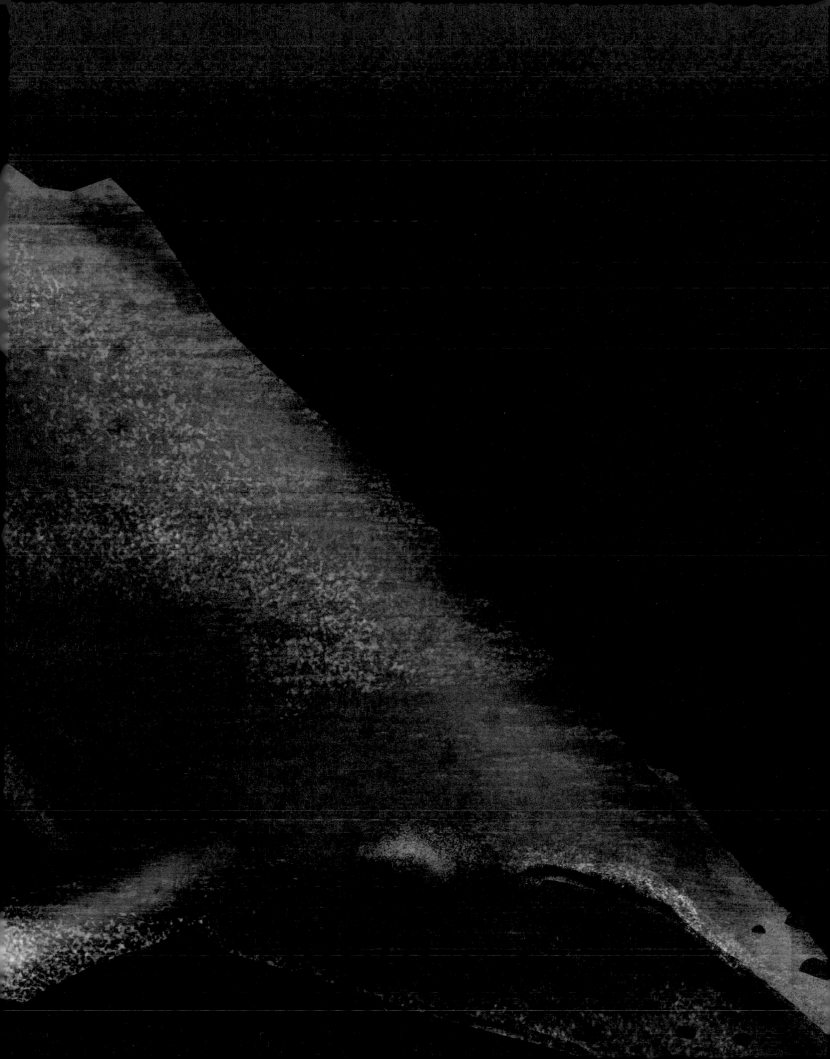

# The Language of Elephants

In the Dzanga-Sangha clearing,
forest elephants cluster at the river.
**Can you hear them?**

Snort

Ruuuummmmble

Roar

Ruuuummmmble

Cry

Ruuuummmmble

Bark

Ruuuummmmble

Baby elephants plunge
trunks into muddy water.
   Can you hear them?

*Spray*
        *Buuubbbllle*
*Splash*
        *Buuubbbllle*
*Grunt*
        *Buuubbbllle*
*Slosh*
        *Buuubbbllle*

Beneath a baobab tree,
a family of elephants speak in soft, low murmurs.

## Can you hear them?

# Forest Orchestra

**PERFORMANCE KEY:** This poem can be performed in multiple ways: all creatures can make their sounds at the same time, each species group can sing together, or readers may experiment with their own ways to perform the poem. Keep in mind that animals have adapted different sound tones so when singing together they don't drown each other out. Birds sing with the highest voice, insects call with a middle tone, and mammals communicate with the lowest sound.

## MAMMALS

red fox: *ow-wow-wow-wow    ow-wow-wow-wow    ow-wow-wow-wow*

American red squirrel: *muk-muk-muk    muk-muk-muk    muk-muk-muk*

chipmunk: *chip-chip-chip    chip-chip-chip    chip-chip-chip*

white-tailed deer fawn: *bleat-bleat-bleat    bleat-bleat-bleat    bleat-bleat-bleat*

## INSECTS

common true katydid: *Ka-ty-did, she didn't, she did    Ka-ty-did, she didn't, she did    Ka-ty-did, she didn't, she did*

Boll's grasshopper: *tst-tst-tst-tst-tst    tst-tst-tst-tst-tst    tst-tst-tst-tst-tst*

Linne's cicada: *zeger-zeger-zeger    zeger-zeger-zeger    zeger-zeger-zeger*

## BIRDS

ovenbird: *teacher    teacher    teacher*

eastern towhee: *Drink-your-TEA    Drink-your-TEA    Drink-your-TEA*

hairy woodpecker: *peek    peek    peek*

black-throated blue warbler: *Please-please-SQUEEZE-me    Please-please-SQUEEZE-me    Please-please-SQUEEZE-me*

blue-gray gnatcatcher: *pzzzz    pzzzz    pzzzz*

black-capped chickadee: *chick-a-dee-dee-dee    chick-a-dee-dee-dee    chick-a-dee-dee-dee*

American robin: *Cheer-up, cheerily    Cheer-up, cheerily    Cheer-up, cheerily*

29

# Nature's Notes

## Animal Songs

The sounds animals make may seem simpler than human sounds, but they have similar purposes. These include communicating hunger, attracting a mate, warning of danger, scaring competitors and predators, establishing a territory, keeping a group together, calling to their young, and conveying the location of food, among other reasons. Not all creatures use their voices to communicate. Some, like crickets and grasshoppers, rub body parts together to make sounds. This action is called stridulation. Fish may fill their swim bladders with air, then contract and expand muscles around the bladder to create sounds. The study of animal sounds (including those of humans) is called bioacoustics.

## We Don't Say *Ribbit*!

Frogs and toads are both amphibians, and toads are actually a type of frog. Frogs, which spend most of their lives near or in water, have moist, slimy skin and long legs for jumping. Toads, which spend more time on land, have dry bumpy skin, and short legs for walking or hopping. To attract a mate, male frogs and toads make sounds by squeezing their lungs and keeping their nostrils and mouths shut. This action forces air over their vocal cords, into their vocal sacs, then back into the lungs for another call. Although at least one species, the Pacific tree frog, does say *ribbit*, most frogs don't. This poem highlights the variety of frog calls. Every species has a distinct one. Even within the same species, there are different dialects, recognizable to others of the same species.

Frogs and toads in order of appearance in the poem: American green tree frog: *quonk*; Fowler's toad: *waaa*; American bullfrog: *jug-o-rum*; eastern narrow-mouthed toad: *beeeee*; spring peeper: *peep*; green frog: *twaang*; eastern spadefoot toad: *errrrgh*; gopher frog: *growl*; American toad: *trill*; pickerel frog: *yeeeeeoooow*.

## We Call to Each Other

We can't see them, but there are invisible highways in the sky called flyways that geese, ducks, and other waterfowl follow when they migrate to warmer climates in the fall, and again when they return to their breeding grounds in the spring. Geese migrate in large groups called flocks and can fly up to 1,500 miles in a day (which is like going from Bangor, Maine, to Cape Canaveral, Florida—a two-day, nonstop drive for a human). Their V-shaped formation creates uplift for the birds that follow, which can reduce the energy they exert by as much as fifty percent. Geese take turns flying in front. Next to humans, geese are the most talkative animals with their characteristic honk. Why are geese so chatty? Scientists say that geese have about two dozen different honks. Some honks are a signal to other geese to take to the air or to pay attention because they'll be landing soon. Others are a way for family members to keep track of one another as they fly. Some are alerts about food or danger. Sometimes when younger geese honk, it seems as if it's simply to show excitement for flying with family and friends.

## Noisy Fish

Lots of fish make sounds. We can't hear them because their sounds are low-pitched and insulated in water, but other fish can hear them. Some fish make sounds by filling an internal sac (swim bladder) with air, then squeezing muscles on or near the sac. This action creates barks, booms, grunts, and more when the air is released. Other fish make sounds by rubbing together skeletal parts or teeth. All fish have ears buried inside their heads. Scientists who studied the ears of various kinds of fish found that fish that live in the deepest, darkest waters (more than one thousand feet down), way beyond the reach of the sun's rays, have specialized ear structures that heighten their hearing. Scientists think that these deep-water fish living in complete darkness have evolved ears, unlike other fish, to help them catch prey, find mates, or evade predators. Fish in order of appearance in the poem: northern puffer: *glub*; crevalle jack: *blub*; longspine squirrelfish: *glug*; silver perch: *swish*; oyster toadfish: *moan*; rock hind: *groan*; longhorn sculpin: *drone*; scrawled cowfish: *grunt*; hardhead catfish: *squeak*; black drum: *boom*; lined seahorse: *tap*; weakfish: *purr*.

## You Can't See Us, but You Can Hear Us

How can an animal the size of a small paper clip fill the air with song? Peepers can be heard on spring evenings calling for a mate from a mile or two away. The male frogs are the singers; vocal sacs under their chins blow up like balloons, letting loose a "peep" when they blow out the air. Peepers typically perform in trios, and the one with the deepest voice usually starts the round.

## Song Thief

The mockingbird sings its melodic songs on warm moonlit spring nights. It spends hours imitating the songs of other birds, but it can also imitate sounds like a barking dog or a whistle. A typical mockingbird has a repertoire of 250 to 350 songs. Scientists believe that mockingbirds imitate the calls of other birds to keep birds from settling in their territory by making it appear as if the area is already heavily populated.

## Rattlesnake Warning

There are around thirty-six species of rattlesnakes around the world, all of which have bony doughnut-like hollow rings on their tails that rattle when they vibrate against one another. A rattlesnake has strong muscles in its tail that can shake the rings at the rate of fifty times per second and for up to three hours. The rattle sound warns other animals, including humans, to stay away. Rattlesnakes can see with their eyes during the day, and at night they have "heat vision." By using heat-sensitive pits, located on either side of their head, they can detect heat given off by animals, which allows them to hunt in the dark and distinguish between prey and predator. Although rattlesnakes rarely bite humans unless threatened, their bite is venomous and is the leading cause of snakebite injuries in North America.

## Cricket Arithmetic

Did you know that you can estimate the temperature outside by counting cricket chirps? If you want to do some cricket arithmetic, go outside in the evening in the spring to late fall when the temperature is above 55 degrees Fahrenheit, stand near an area where crickets live—tall grasses, a field, or the edge of a forest—and listen carefully. It might be difficult, but try to pick out the chirping sound of a single cricket. Count how many chirps the cricket makes in fourteen seconds, write the number

down, then add forty to it. This calculation should give you the approximate temperature in degrees Fahrenheit. Check the temperature on an outdoor thermometer. How close is your estimate? Accuracy will vary according to the type of cricket; the snowy tree cricket is cited as the most precise. This method, known as Dolbear's Law, is a simplified version of the one first formulated by scientist Amos Dolbear in the late 1800s. Crickets chirp faster in hotter weather and slower as the temperature cools. That's because they're cold-blooded and they adopt the temperature of their surrounding environment. When the temperature falls, the cricket's energy level falls causing their chirping to slow down. Only male crickets chirp and they do so by rubbing their wings together using a special structure on the tops of their wings known as a scraper. To chirp, they raise their wings and draw the scraper of one wing across the underside of the other. Female crickets listen for the males' chirping to find a mate, using ears that are located below their knees. But you can use cricket serenades to help calculate the temperature outside.

## Flight of the Honeybees

When honeybees fly, their wing beats make a sound that the human ear hears as buzzing. Worker bees, which are all female and are the largest group of bees in the hive, collect nectar. They use a long tube-shaped tongue to suck the nectar up from the flower and store it in a "honey stomach" located in their throats. When their honey stomachs are full, they fly back to their hive. There, waiting workers begin the process of turning the nectar into honey by fanning it with their wings to evaporate excess water. Scientists have discovered that when honeybees find flowers that hold a lot of nectar they mark them with a sugary scent. Returning to the hive, they perform one of three dances on the honeycomb—a round dance, a sickle dance, or a waggle dance—which, like a map, communicates to other bees the distance and whereabouts of the flowers with the most nectar.

## Bigclaw Snapping Shrimp

Although the snapping shrimp measures just one to two inches long, it makes a sound that is louder than a jet engine. It's one of the loudest creatures on earth along with beluga and sperm whales. A snapping shrimp has one ordinary sized claw and one claw that's larger than half of its body size. The snapping shrimp hides in a burrow when hunting. With a snap, its large claw releases a jet of water at speeds of nearly sixty miles per hour, generating a bubble that can stun its prey (usually a crab or small fish). The popping of the bubble causes the loud sound and creates a flash of light that indicates a burst of heat almost as hot as the sun. There are many different species of snapping shrimp on Earth. They live in colonies in seagrass flats, coral reefs, and oyster reefs.

## Songsters of the Sea

In the 1950s, scientists in Hawaii discovered that whales made sounds under the sea. They heard whales creak, grunt, and make long moans that sounded like songs. Noted biologist Roger Payne pronounced the humpback whale the "Songster of the Sea" after hearing its songs. No one knows for sure why humpback whales sing, but scientists have a few theories: male whales might sing to attract females during mating season, or as a kind of sound guide during migration, or even to bond with other males as support during the breeding season. Both male and female humpback whales make sounds, but only males produce organized songs with melodies and themes that they may repeat dozens of times over several hours. These songs can be heard from more than a thousand miles away. Humpback whales dive anywhere from about 50 feet to over 300 feet beneath the surface of the ocean and sing while suspended below. Unlike humans, whales have no vocal cords and when they sing their mouths don't move. Scientists think that their singing comes from circulating air back and forth through the respiratory system.

## The Language of Elephants

Elephants speak with two voices—they speak through their mouths or from the end of their trunks. Depending on which method they use, their rumbles, grunts, and cries are different. But most of what elephants say to each other is infrasonic, which means the sounds are too low for human ears to hear. Elephants are intensely social and can communicate with other elephants up to ten miles away. In the Dzanga-Sangha Special Reserve of the Central African Republic, scientists are working on the Elephant Listening Project. They're recording and interpreting the meaning of over seventy different elephants' rumbles and low-frequency sounds with a goal of creating an "elephant dictionary."

## Forest Orchestra

The sounds of the forest in the summer are like an animal orchestra. Birds sing, insects *tst*, and larger animals *bleat* and *chip*. Scientists studying soundscape ecology noticed that in places like a forest where multiple animals "talk" at the same time, their sounds are not chaotic as might be expected. They discovered that animals have adapted to create a kind of orchestra. Whether animals are trying to attract a mate or warn of danger or make noise for any other reason, they need to call at a pitch that will allow their sounds to be heard amongst the many others in the forest. Insects evolved a variety of sounds to avoid being drowned out by others. Birds rise above insects' calls by singing at a higher pitch, and birds with shorter calls fit in between the calls of birds with longer ones. Frogs puncture the buzzing insect noise with short, loud bursts. Mammals call at both high and low frequencies. Animals have also evolved to be heard over sounds of thunder, wind, gushing rivers, and in more recent history, the sounds of human civilization. All the animals communicating in this poem live in the northeastern American forest.